D0832488

Wordle: The Rules, Strategy and Expert Tips

From Novice to Expert in Less than 60 Minutes

Mary S. Schaeffer

Copyright © 2022 Mary S. Schaeffer

All rights reserved.

ISBN: 978-1-7351000-5-0

TABLE OF CONTENTS

Wordle: The Rules, Strategy and Expert Tips

1 WHAT IS WORDLE

Wordle is a fun and free game sweeping the Internet. It is only available online. Very simply put; you are given six chances to guess the five-letter word of the day. While at first glance it may seem intimidating, it is anything but, once you know the few simple rules. And they are quite easy to execute.

The beauty of the game, at least for me, is that there is only one word released each day. So, you can get on your computer to play Wordle in the morning, or whenever, and not worry about going down the rabbit hole where hours upon hours disappear.

How often have you said to yourself, as you open your favorite game, 'I'll just play one hand,' and then two or three hours later, you find yourself still glued to your computer. That won't happen with Wordle.

The game was developed by a software engineer, Josh Wardle, for his partner. This might give you a clue as to how the name of the game was created. It is a variation of the creator's name. We owe him a big thank you for sharing this delightful diversion

Wordle: The Rules, Strategy and Expert Tips

with the community at large.

Once the game was released to the public, it quickly became an obsession with many. Newspapers like the New York Times, USA Today and many, many others carried articles about this compelling game. Talk show hosts, both late night and during the day, featured the game.

How popular is Wordle? According to the Daily Mail in the UK, on November 1, 2021, there were 90 people playing it. In early January, after opening it up to the world, more than 300,000 were playing. That number is now believed to be in the millions. And it's spreading.

It quickly became a trending topic. There are a few other features that make this such an attractive diversion:

- The one-per-day limit

- The website has no advertising, and if published reports are to be believed, there will never be any advertising on the page

- If you follow a few simply guidelines, which we will outline in this book, you can win almost every time.

- After you finish your hand for the day, the website pops up a link that you can share on social media. So, if you wish, you can brag on social media; but don't tell what the day's answer is. That's just bad form and ruins it for others.

To help with your Wordleing, we've included some blank note pages at the end. [Yes, I made that word up.]

Here's what I saw after my first two games, before I had the embarrassment of not winning a hand.

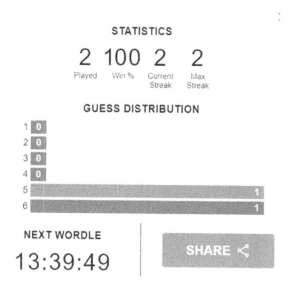

We've got some diagrams through-out this book, because I am really a believer that sometimes a picture is really worth 1,000 words. However, it is in black and white in the print version of the book and you won't see the famed green and mustard yellow boxes. We could have done the book in color, but the cost would have been prohibitive and we wanted as many people as possible to have access to it.

I want to make one last point as we work our way through the intricacies of Wordle. There are no short cuts or cheating in this book. The game is a game of wits, a challenge for yourself. If we gave tips on cheating, that would defeat the whole purpose of playing, at least that's how I see it.

Well, that's enough of me waxing poetic about Wordle, let's move on and learn how to play the game.

2 HOW TO PLAY WORDLE

The rules are pretty simple. Here they are:

- You have six chances to guess the five-letter word of the day.
- Every word that is entered, must be a legitimate word. If it's not, Wordle won't let you enter it.
- When you key in the word, you must hit the enter key for Wordle to recognize it. [It took me several minutes to realize that!].
- If a letter in the word you entered is correct AND is in the right location, it will turn green.
- If a letter you enter in the word is correct but not in the right location, it will turn a mustard yellow.
- If the letter you enter in the word is not in the final answer, it will stay gray.

That's it. It's that simple. Once you've entered the first word and can see what's what, you can then judiciously, select the second word.

Again, like the first time out, it must be a legitimate word. This can be seriously annoying, when you are trying to use a few letters and they don't seem to go together in a legitimate word.

Let's take a look at a recent example.

Before we get to that, here's the website where the game is currently hosted:

https://www.powerlanguage.co.uk/wordle/

Tip #1: the first time you go to this page, the site has some basic instructions. Click on the little x, to make them disappear.

Tip #2: If the owners of the game have to move it at some point and you go to that page and it's not there, do a simple google search to find it.

Here's what the screen looks like before you enter any letters.

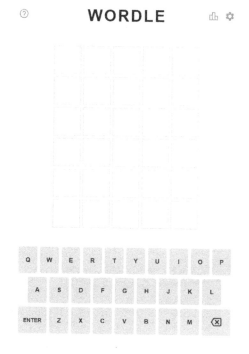

Wordle: The Rules, Strategy and Expert Tips

The first few times I played, I didn't bother doing any planning or thinking about what to start with. I knew that S and T were very common letters in the words in the English language. I also suspected that most five letter words would have two vowels. So I started with the word STAIR. As you'll see in the next chapter, this was an okay place to start, but not the very best. But let's see what happened with STAIR. This was one of my first games.

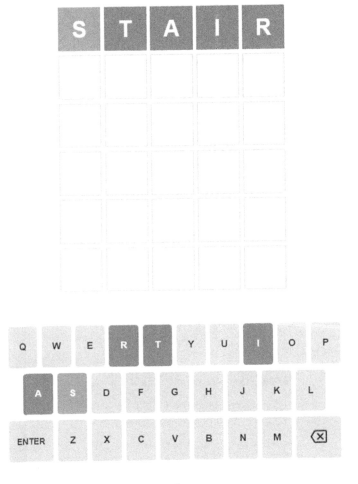

Wordle: The Rules, Strategy and Expert Tips

What happened here, which you probably can't tell so well because this book is printed in black and white, is that the S showed up green. So, the S is correct and in the right place.

The other letters, are now showing in a darker gray. That's to remind you that you used them and they weren't correct. So, don't use them again.

Of course, you can use them again; but that's just throwing away part of your chance at a right guess, because Wordle isn't going to change its mind midway through the game. Wrong is wrong.

Because this was my first game, and I hadn't given much thought to strategy, I made a terrible choice for the second guess, as shown below.

As you can see, none of the letters were part of the final solution. As you will see in the next chapter, I actually made a really poor choice. But I did find out which letters weren't in the final solution and that helped a little.

By focusing on the vowels, I had eliminated A, E and I from the final mix. So, I needed a word, I thought, with an O. That's why I chose BLOOM.

This time I got lucky. I picked up two letters, the L and the M. The L was in the right spot and the M was the right letter but it was in the wrong spot.

At this point I knew several things, (in addition to the growing group of letters NOT in the correct solution. You can surmise that:

- The correct answer starts with an SL

- The M is in the fourth spot. We know it's not in the last spot, and the first two spots are spoken for. The odds are high, possibly even 100% that the third letter is a vowel.
- The third spot is probably a vowel and the only vowel missing is U

What word starts with SLUM? There are actually two- and I picked the wrong one the first time. I tried SLUMS and it wasn't right. Here's what my final screen looked like.

The correct answer was SLUMP.

After that, to my great horror, I lost two games. After those humiliating failures, it became obvious to me, I needed to develop a strategy, especially for that all important word. And, that's what I did and am sharing it with you

3 STARING AT THE BLANK SCREEN: THE BEST STARTING WORD

Because of my math background, I knew immediately that the most likely words were the ones that would have the most common letters of the alphabet in them. So, that's where I started. I want to explain how I went about finding the best starting word, the one that will give you the best chance of winning this game. The reason for going into so much detail is that if you understand my reasoning, you'll be well positioned not only to pick the right starting word, but to go on and make a good choice for your second word etc.

But not to worry, I'm going to avoid talking about two things:

- The mathematics behind the probabilities for my selections. I suspect most people would find that as mind-numbing as I do when my husband tries to explain to me what was wrong with my computer and how he fixed it. [zzzzz]

- The coding behind the game. Probably for the same reason above PLUS I don't understand it myself, so am in no position to say anything intelligent on that matter.

But I am going to share a few numbers with you. And they relate to the frequency of the use of various letters of the alphabet. The list below shows the letters listed in order of their frequency, or popularity. So, for example, looking at the list below, we can see that a word is far more likely to have an E or an A in it than a Q or J. Probably not a big surprise.

1. E
2. A
3. R
4. I
5. O
6. T
7. N
8. S
9. L
10. C
11. U
12. D
13. P
14. M
15. H
16. G
17. B
18. F
19. Y
20. W
21. K
22. V
23. X

24. Z
25. J
26. Q

Now, if Wordle didn't have the requirement that all guesses be legitimate English words, our best bet would be to enter EARIO as our first choice. That would provide the best chance at having the most correct letters.

But there is a second problem, in addition to the issue of only using legitimate English words. EARIO has four vowels. Most five-letter words will only have two vowels. So, focus on words with two vowels for your first choice.

Tip #3: Start with words with two vowels. Since E and A are the top two letters on the list, in addition to being vowels, always include them in your first choice.

Looking back at the list, you can see that the first three consonants are R S and N. The problem with that is there is no legitimate word with the letters E A R S and N. So, I suggest you discard the least popular N and replace it with the next letter on the list, T.

When you do that, you get the very legitimate TEARS or perhaps STARE. You can use either, but I have a slight preference for TEARS because it gives you a shot at S in the last spot and many words end in an S given that it is the plural of many four-letter words.

Of course, some of you are probably thinking, but a lot of words ends in E, and you have a point.

Here's a game I played recently using my new strategy of starting with T E A R S.

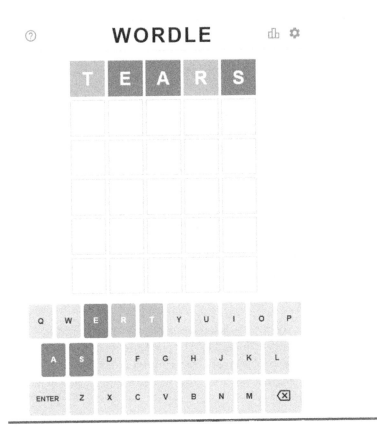

I got lucky on this one in that I got both the R and the T, but they weren't in the right place.

I knew that without any vowels, I had to go hunting for them on the next try. So, I needed a word that had an I and an O. I also had to try and find the right location for the R and T. Since I was trying not to spend too long on the game, I was only able to try a new position for the T, while checking out I and O. I used the word POINT.

I hit the jackpot. The T was now in the right place and I found my vowel and in the correct place; the O was in the second spot. I still needed to figure out where the R went. But that was now narrowed down to two places, either the first or third spot. I tried the first spot and was rewarded.

Working my way down the list of letter popularity, I was looking for a word with B and L. I came up with BLAME, trying to see if they were viable options.

I got this.

For a minute I was stumped. The answer contained a B, but it could only be in the third or fourth spot. I couldn't imagine any words ending in BT, so it must go in the middle. That just left the fourth spot. It took me a minute to figure it out, but all of the sudden, a light went off. Did you figure it out?

Try looking at this:

R O B _ T

Does that help?

Wordle: The Rules, Strategy and Expert Tips

I saw all greens when I typed in my answer. The correct answer was ROBOT. That's when I realized, the same letter might be used more than once in a word and that was another factor to take into consideration.

Let's take a look at some other popular starting words that contain A and E. They include:

- ASTER
- RATES
- RESAT
- STARE
- TARES
- TEARS

Tip #4: Start with any of the words above. This will give you a leg up on discovering the vowels in the word, while at the same time helping you focus on the popular consonants.

Any of these will probably work just as well as TEARS. I use TEARS for a very simple reason; it was the first word that came to mind when I tried to make a word from the given letters.

4 WORDLE STRATEGY: GETTING TO THE FINISH LINE IN LESS THAN SIX MOVES—MAYBE

Did you notice that the word MAYBE has five letters in it and it contains an A and an E? That would make it a decent starting word, but not ideal, IMHO. But I digress.

Let's take a look at a logical way to play the game—and a way that should help you win, most, if not all of the time.

Step 1: Start with one of your optimum words, ideally one containing the most popular letters as discussed in the prior chapter.

Step 2.a: Once you get the results, evaluate what you have. If you don't have any vowels, try a word with an I and an O. Following the best practice of using the most common letters of the alphabet, not already tested, you'd use a word from the letters I O N C L. Alas, once again, there are no words.

So, let's replace the last letter on the list, the L, with the next letter and see if we can find some words. When the C is replaced with an L, there is only one possibility and that is INDOL. If you are wondering what it is, as I was, here's the definition:

> a white or yellowish crystalline heterocyclic compound extracted from coal tar and used in perfumery, medicine, and as a flavoring agent.

Step 2.b: When you evaluate the results from step 1, if you only get one vowel, you might try the recommendation in Step 2.a. This is because most, but definitely not all, five-letter words will have two vowels. And of course, there is the chance that the vowel will be repeated. There is one other option for a one-vowel word. And that is that there is a Y in the word, probably at the end.

Step 2.c: When you evaluate the results from step 1, if you have two vowels, you want to focus now on

A) Getting the vowels in the right spot and

B) Finding the right consonants.

Step 3: Be strategic with each of your choices. Make educated guesses, based on the information you have already uncovered and letters that appear more frequently.

Tip#5: If after two chances, you have eliminated A E I and O and are still having trouble with the consonants, don't bother guessing U, until you are close to the end. You need to reserve your choices to find some of your consonants and place them in the right position.

Tip#6: Don't forget to use your power of deduction. Let's look at a simple case. Let's say you have a C and you know it is in the last place and you also have a P and you don't know where it goes. Clearly, it can't go in the fourth spot. Don't waste time and guesses putting it there.

I want to share one more example, that might have looked kind of hopeless in the beginning. I got it on the third try. But don't be too impressed. When you see how I figured it out, you'll realize there was a little bit of luck and some common sense.

This is where I stood after two rounds. It was before I had found the magic second word of INDOL (which wouldn't have helped 😊. I knew I wanted a word with O and I and there was the L.

So, I used LOINS, even though it meant using a letter that was definitely wrong. The diagram shows that the solution contains an R, but not in fourth place and an I in third place.

Here's what I deduced after studying the diagram for a bit.

- It was unlikely that the word contained a U.

- It was unlikely that the I was repeated twice, definitely not in the second or fourth position.

- It was unlikely that the R was in last position.

- The word started with consonant cluster or blend, making it likely the R was in second position.

- I then decided that the first three letters were probably PRI. In looking at this afterwards, I realize they could have also been FRI. [Remember, T had been eliminated in the first round, so the solution definitely did not start with TRI.

And that's when I came up with the solution, in only three rounds.

Before you turn the page to uncover the winning solution for that day, take a minute and try and figure out what you'd guess.

5 DON'T GET DISCOURAGED: ANOTHER EXAMPLE … THAT STARTED OFF QUITE POORLY

Six chances to guess a five-letter word! It seems like the odds would be against you, especially if you aren't particularly successful in the first two rounds.

This is another example before I found INDOL. Here's what I was looking at after two rounds. It was not looking like this would be a winning hand

All I had managed to identify in the first round was the R and in the second round I found the right place for the R, but still no vowels and only the one lonely consonant. But that's not really all I knew. I also had discovered:

- The word did not contain an A, E or O.

- It did it contain the popular letters T S D and N.

Since I appeared in more words than U, I decided to focus on a word that included the I. Since I knew the R had to be in the second spot, I decided the word likely started with one of those consonant blends, like TR, FR, PR, CR or GR. Since the T had been eliminated in the first round, that further improved my odds. I went with the GR because it was the first one I thought of. If I was strictly following the rules and had my little chart in front of me, I might have gone with the PR. But I really couldn't come up with too many five-letter words starting with PRI.

So, I went with the following:

And my logic partially paid off. I now knew what the middle three letters were. I went back and looked at my consonant blends and decided to try the PR. Note: I probably should have used that the first time. That seemed the most likely. I was rewarded but not in the way I expected. Here's what I saw.

The P was a correct letter but in the wrong spot! It had to go in the last spot. So, I started going through the alphabet in my head. It didn't take me long to come up with the following.

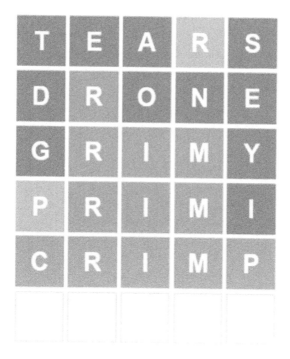

Crimp was the right word. Not something that was at all on my mind, when I had identified that first R.

There's one last point I want to make about going through the alphabet when you are missing only one letter and you know where it is located.

This example also demonstrates that you shouldn't give up if at the beginning it looks hopeless. It can take just one or two letters to turn the whole situation around.

Tip#7: When you have only one letter left and you know what spot it goes in and you start going through the alphabet in your mind, don't necessarily jump at the first correct response. Sometimes there is more than one option and you want to select the best one, not necessarily the first one that comes into your mind.

6 OTHER WORDLE STRATEGIES

Not everyone uses the popular letter strategy discussed earlier in this work. There is a group of Wordle aficionados who focus on the vowels exclusively at the start of their games.

The Vowel Approach

They use this approach this be starting with words that are rich in vowels, i.e., have three or four vowels in the word. As you probably have figured out, there are no five-letter words that have all five vowels in them. Some of those words include:

- Adieu
- Audio – doesn't have the most popular letter, E
- Miaou – doesn't have the most popular letter, E
- Aurei
- Ourie – doesn't have the second most popular letter A
- Uraei

If you have no idea what the last four mean, join the club. But they do work with Wordle.

There are also a number of words with three vowels. According to the Internet, there are 835 such words. We're not going to list them all here. However, if you are looking to start with a vowel rich word, here are a few that you might consider:

- Alive
- Olive
- Abide
- Irate
- Email
- Adore
- Aside
- Alike
- Aisle
- Douse

If I were to choose one of these, I would definitely pick one that included and E and an A. I'd also choose one with the more common consonants. IRATE would be one good choice.

The Popular Word Endings

We've already mentioned consonant clusters but have only focused on them at the beginning of a word. Likewise, there are some other common features for word endings. Let's take a look at a few. Common word endings include:

- ING
- ED
- LY
- ION
- AL

There are more endings, but given that Wordle focuses on five-letter words, they aren't realistic alternatives for winning selections for the game. While, word endings aren't as critical as vowels to finding the solution quickly, they should be taken into accounts when facing an odd selection of letters.

7 WORDLE: DOUBLE LETTERS

Without a doubt, the same letter can appear twice in the correct Wordle answers. This can happen in a variety of ways. Recent correct responses included ROBOT and ABBEY. The reason this issue stumps so many players is that when they enter the letter as a guess, it will appear green or yellow, depending on whether it is in the correct location.

Most people then move onto other letters forgetting that just because they have one correct response using that letter, doesn't mean it isn't in there a second time. And the only way Wordle will let you know is if you enter it a second time.

When this happened to me with ABBEY, I was stunned when I saw the correct answer, as I had never considered it. The second time, with ROBOT, I got it. I had four of the five letters and it was fairly obvious where they went. I literally had the four letters up there and only when working through all the vowels, did I hit on the correct answer.

Consecutive letters happen occasionally as follows:

- When it comes to vowels, O is the most likely to be double right next to each other, as for example, goody. The only other double vowel is EE and it occurs once.

- When it comes to consonants, BB and LL are the most common, although not really common at all.

It's the non-consecutive doubles that are cause the most problems. We're so intent on finding the right letters, we sometimes forget about them.

Note: Wordle doesn't alert you that the word contains a double letter. The only way to find it is to put the letter in twice yourself.

Tip #8: If you're stumped, look back over the letters that you already know are in the solution and see if any of them make sense for as a double; remembering they don't have to be consecutive.

Here's a recent example, and I thought for a while I was in trouble. Here's what it looked like after the first round when I used my magic first word.

That's right, my magic word failed me. None of the most popular letters were in the solution anywhere. I had better luck in the second round.

This time I struck gold. Not only were the N and the L in the final solution, I had them in the correct spots. The O was also in the final solution, but not in the spot I had it. It must be either in the first spot or the third spot.

I was convinced it was in the first spot, (for reasoning that as you will see was completely incorrect and so I won't share it with you) and decided to use the next round to see if I could sort out any of the other letters. I thought that would help because I hadn't a clue with what I was staring at, and I was spending far too much time coming up with nothing. I'll grant you, my next choice wasn't stellar, but it did help eliminate some of the more common letters.

At this point I was still convinced the O belonged in the first spot, and so I set out to test that thesis, figuring if I could see the word with three of the five letters in the right spot, it would come to me. I was 100% wrong, but I did now know where the O belonged.

I was a little startled at this result. I now knew the correct response would look like

_ N O _ L. I kept trying to sound out different words. I was playing around with a Y as the fourth letter and the results were even more bizarre. And, that was only after playing around with _ N O O L.

Up until this point, I'd forgotten about silent letters. Once I remembered silent letters, the solution was obvious. Take a moment before reading on to see if you can come up with the correct answer.

Did you get it right?

8 FINE TUNING YOUR GAME: WORDLE STRATEGIES TO FURTHER IMPROVE YOUR ODDS

While there's no surefire way to guarantee you'll win Wordle every single time, there are some tactics you can use to improve your odds greatly. That's the purpose of this chapter. But before we get to that, I want to share why I believe it is impossible to guarantee that someone can win every single time.

Consider this example. You've gotten four of the five letters. They are O L L Y. Now, unless you are just taking wild guesses, and not following common sense approaches to the game, I maintain that it will take you at least two guesses to get there, probably more, given the double L. That leaves you four chances.

You might be feeling pretty good, like you've definitely got this nailed, this is one hand you can't lose. Your options are:

- Dolly

- Folly

- Jolly

- Molly

- Tolly

I'm going to be honest, I also thought lolly, (short for lollipop) was a word, but spell check tells me it is not a valid word. But I digress.

There are five choices, but you only have four (or less) left. So, no guaranteed win. You can probably come up with some more examples. This is why I say, following the tips in this book and below will increase your odds, but never guarantee a win.

So, on to the additional tactics that will **almost** guarantee you a win in each and every hand.

- Consider this: The English language has over 400,000 words. Of those, only about 10% start with a vowel. So, to increase your odds of winning, focus your initial guesses on words that start with a consonant.

- Remember, most five-letter words have two vowels, and if they don't, they probably have a Y. Keep in mind, that the two vowels may be the same, as in ROBOT.

- Even though the program is hosted on a UK site, the word spellings are all America. So, center, not centre, and authorize, not authorize. [Yes, I know those aren't five letter words, just trying to make the point.]

Wordle: The Rules, Strategy and Expert Tips

- Start with one of the popular words that includes as many of the most-frequently-used letters of the alphabet; not your lucky word or favorite word or whatever.

- Avoid starting with the words that include letters least used in the alphabet. These include Z K W X. You may use them later, as you narrow down your search, but don't start with them.

- Never use a Q, unless you already know that the U is one of the letters.

- With only a few exceptions, if a Q is in the word, it is in first position.

- When dealing with I and E, remember the old adage from your grammar school days. It goes I before E, except after C, when sounded like A as in neighbor and weigh.

- Here's one, I'll bet most of those reading this didn't know. There are over 7500 words that end in K, and only 2145, that start with K. So, if you identify K as one of the letters in your answer, the odds are high it is at the end of the word. If there's a C and K, make sure to try something ending in CK, to start.

- When it comes to the letter Z, it is unlikely to be at the start of the word. It is more likely to be somewhere in the middle of the word or the end of the word. So, if you identify Z as one of the letters in your answer, the least likely location is the beginning. Well, okay, it's probably not the second or next to last spot either.

Wordle: The Rules, Strategy and Expert Tips

- Don't forget the words that have been recent winners. It is unlikely, but probably not impossible, that those words will be the correct choice for the winning word.

- Silent letters abound in the English language. So, while trying to sound out potential solutions is one good strategy when you are almost at the end of the game and are only missing one or two letters, it will miss some good solutions. Some common silent letters include leading K, as in KNOLL, Knitting etc., D in words such as HEDGE and WEDGE. Then there is G, often found in combination with an H. Some examples include WEIGHT and MIGHT. There are many other examples.

- Don't get discouraged and give up if you get only one letter (in the wrong place) or none, with your first guess. The whole game can come together with your second, third and sometimes even fourth selection.

.

9 WORDLE WORST PRACTICES

There are some things you can do that will really impede your chances of winning your game. Most of them should be obvious, but, just in case they're not, let's take a look at a few.

Worst Practice #1: Starting with words that contain the least popular letters of the alphabet. These include words that contain:

- Q
- J
- Z
- X
- V
- K

And of course, the vowel U. Avoid these words until you have other data that will help you make an educated guess about the right choice.

Worst Practice #2: Repeating a letter already entered without a definite plan. If you think it has a chance of being a double, or it's the only way to enter another set of letters that you want to enter, then go for it. But without a set plan, it's a waste of a chance.

Worst Practice #3: Forgetting that the letter Y sometimes masquerades as a vowel. So, when you're stumped and have run out of feasible vowel options, don't forget to try Y as a vowel.

Worst Practice #4: Learn not only from what you see, but what you can infer from each round. A simple example of this might be the following. If you learn in your playing that A E I and U are not in the final answer, the odds are very high that the correct answer contains an O.

Worst Practice #5: Revealing the correct answer for the day on social media before the day is over. This is just bad form and has the potential to ruin it for other players. You will notice that the link Wordle gives you to share your results, does not include the right answer, or for that matter, any of the letters. It just shows whether your responded correctly or not. So, be a good member of the Wordle community and keep the correct answer to yourself until the end of the day.

10 WORDLE FOR ADVANCED PLAYERS

Yes, there is an advanced version of Wordle. You might want to try this if you are getting the right answer on a regular basis, especially if you want to challenge yourself.

In the advanced version, you kind of have fewer choices. Once you identify a letter as being in the final solution, you must use it in every guess, you make. And, if you have it in the correct place, i.e., you not only identified the correct letter but the correct location, your guesses must have it in the correct location.

What this does, is remove the option to try different words at the second and third round trying to identify letters included but not using the letters you already know.

So, let's say your first guess was CHAPS. When you hit the enter key, you learn that the final solution has an H in the second spot and has a P, albeit not in the fourth spot. Every guess after that must have the H in the second spot and a P. Yes, really annoying. In this case, not a real WORDLE example I might add, the correct answer is PHONE.

So, where is this version of Wordle. It's at exactly the same spot regular Wordle is.

 # WORDLE

Simply click on the settings icon (shown above by the arrow) and change it to Hard. You will note you can also change the settings there if you are Color Blind. You can also change the screen background color to black in the same spot.

Whatever changes you make, if you decide you don't want to continue in that mode, make sure to change them back when you finish.

You will also notice on the diagram, the bar chart widget. This will give you your current stats for the game played on that machine and on that browser. And lastly, if you want to review the instructions, click on the question mark, and they will pop up again.

11 A FEW LAST WORDS: MORE WORDLE

This book is a departure from what I normally write about. It's also a lot shorter. 😊 It is meant to be a quick read.

The book is meant as a companion to the Wordle content carried on YouTube and as part of the AP Now podcast. We release new Wordle video and podcast on Saturday mornings at 9 AM ET. You can access them:

- On YouTube at www.YouTube at www.youtube.com/c/APNow

- Wherever you listen to podcasts by searching for AP Now

- And, they have their own playlist at https://www.ap-now.com/snip/110.htm

Typically, I cover issues impacting the payments and accounts payable function for professionals who work in, manage or have responsibility for those areas. That is done through AP Now and includes a membership website, several webinars a month, a monthly newsletter, some books, a free twice-a-week ezine, and a podcast, that is also carried on YouTube.

If you have anything to do with the payment or accounts payable functions, please check out some of our other videos and consider joining our community by signing up for our free ezine. You can do that at www.ap-now.com by using the box to the top left, or simply wait 5 seconds and a drop-down box will appear.

Finally, thanks for sticking through until the end. If you liked this book, a four-or-five-star rating and or review on Amazon and/or Goodreads is very much appreciated.

Good luck and Enjoy

Mary S. Schaeffer
@MarySSchaeffer on Twitter
www.youtube.com/c/APNow
https://podcasts.apple.com/us/podcast/apnow/id1459045697
https://www.audible.com/pd/APNow-Podcast/B08K568S26

ABOUT THE AUTHOR

Mary S. Schaeffer, founder of AP Now and host of the AP Now podcast, is the author of 21 books, most of which are focused on accounts payable and payment issues. She is the recipient of a Lifetime Achievement award and the Well Being for Others award from the AP Association, a global organization headquartered in the UK.

In her spare time, she is an avid reader (mostly mysteries), Board member (and former Treasurer) for the Gesneriad Society, Life Master in the ACBL and devourer of Sudoku puzzles. She shares her home with her husband and well over 300 house plants.

Wordle Notes

Wordle Notes

Wordle: The Rules, Strategy and Expert Tips

Wordle Notes

Wordle Notes

Wordle Notes

Wordle Notes

Wordle Notes

Wordle Notes

Wordle Notes

Wordle Notes

Wordle Notes

Wordle Notes

Wordle Notes

Wordle Notes

Wordle Notes

Wordle Notes

Wordle Notes

Wordle Notes

Wordle Notes

Wordle Notes

Wordle Notes

Wordle Notes

Wordle Notes

Wordle Notes

Wordle Notes

Wordle Notes

Wordle Notes

Wordle Notes

Wordle Notes

Wordle Notes

Wordle Notes

Wordle Notes

Wordle Notes

Wordle Notes

Wordle Notes

Wordle Notes

Wordle Notes

Wordle Notes

Wordle Notes

Wordle Notes

Wordle Notes

Wordle Notes

Wordle Notes

Wordle Notes

Wordle Notes

Wordle Notes